The Storekeeper

Pamela McDowell

Weigl

Published by Weigl Educational Publishers Limited
6325 10th Street SE
Calgary, Alberta
T2H 2Z9

Website: www.weigl.ca

Library and Archives Canada Cataloguing in Publication

McDowell, Pamela, author
The Storekeeper / Pamela McDowell.

(Early Canadians)
Includes index.
ISBN 978-1-77071-888-3 (bound).--ISBN 978-1-77071-889-0 (pbk.)

    1. General stores--Canada--History--Juvenile literature.
2. Frontier and pioneer life--Canada--Juvenile literature. I. Title.
II. Title: Stores and storekeepers. III. Series: Early Canadians (Calgary, Alta.)

HF5429.6.C3M38 2013   j381.0971   C2013-902404-2

Printed in the United States of America in North Mankato, Minnesota
1 2 3 4 5 6 7 8 9 0 17 16 15 14 13

062013
WEP130613

Project Coordinator: Megan Cuthbert
Design: Terry Paulhus

Photograph Credits
Weigl acknowledges Getty Images, Glenbow Museum, and Library and Archives
Canada as the primary image suppliers for this title.

Every reasonable effort has been made to trace ownership and to obtain
permission to reprint copyright material. The publishers would be pleased to
have any errors or omissions brought to their attention so that they may be
corrected in subsequent printings.

We acknowledge the financial support of the Government of Canada through
the Canada Book Fund for our publishing activities.

CONTENTS

Introduction 4

Life of a Storekeeper 6

A Storekeeper's Tools........................8

In the Morning...................................10

Goods for Sale 12

Lunch Time..14

Cash, Trade, or Credit 16

Closing Time 18

Christmas...20

Storekeepers Today...........................22

Then and Now Diagram 23

Glossary/Index 24

The storekeeper was an important person in a town. People depended on the storekeeper to sell items they could not make or grow on their farms. Often, storekeepers opened a store soon after the first pioneers settled in an area. Storekeepers sold **goods** out of a tent until a store could be built from logs.

Early general stores were sometimes made from tents and packing crates.

Solid walls and a roof protected the goods from bad weather and animals. Later, storekeepers might build a **false front** onto the store. The false front had big windows and made the store look larger and more successful. As the town grew, the store grew, too.

As a community grew, the storekeeper offered more goods for sale.

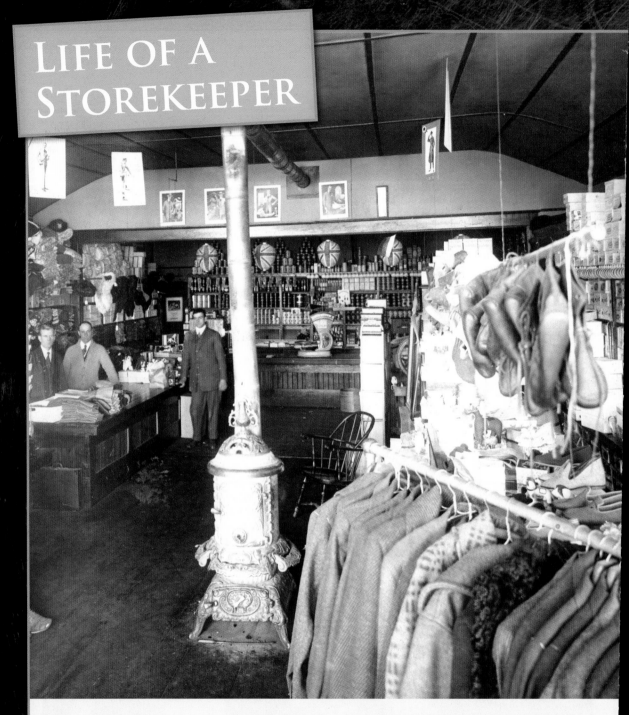

LIFE OF A STOREKEEPER

S torekeepers were busy from early morning until night. They got to know everyone who lived in the town and on the farms nearby. The store was the **hub** of the community. Some people stopped by to visit with each other and with the storekeeper. Others dropped off letters and packages for the mail.

The store was often a family business. The storekeeper's family usually lived upstairs or at the back of the store. Sometimes, the storekeeper worked very late, so it was helpful to live close by.

The storekeeper had few tools when the store was first opened. Goods were often sold from packing crates until a proper place for business could be built. Storekeepers did not have scanners or computers like stores use today. The storekeeper used a few simple tools to keep track of what was sold.

Cash box

At first, the storekeeper kept money in a simple wooden box. Later, a metal cabinet with drawers for coins and bills was used. In the 1880s, storekeepers started using cash registers. Cash registers helped the storekeeper add up the cost of the items a person wanted to buy.

Account book

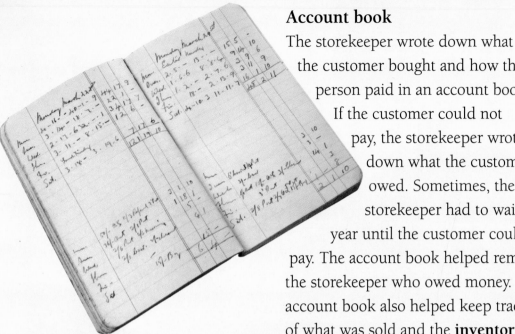

The storekeeper wrote down what the customer bought and how the person paid in an account book. If the customer could not pay, the storekeeper wrote down what the customer owed. Sometimes, the storekeeper had to wait a year until the customer could pay. The account book helped remind the storekeeper who owed money. The account book also helped keep track of what was sold and the **inventory** of goods in the store.

Scale

Skilled storekeepers could use their hands to estimate the weight of some items. Sometimes, a customer needed to buy an exact amount of something. The storekeeper used a scale to weigh items that were sold in **bulk**, such as flour and sugar. There were different scales to weigh food, mail, and hardware products.

In the Morning

BOWDEN

Many storekeepers built stores near railway lines so they could serve more people.

The storekeeper was up by 7:00 am to start the day. The first task was to take the mail to the train station. The storekeeper returned to the store to cut and chop wood for the stove. The chopped wood was also sold to customers.

The female storekeeper started the fire in the stove and kept it burning all day. She spent the entire day working in the store. She tidied the counter, stocked shelves, and helped customers.

GOODS FOR SALE

Settlers depended on the storekeeper for items they could not grow or make themselves, such as coffee and shoes. The settlers also bought blankets, fabric, wool clothing, mining tools, and pots and pans. They bought foods such as flour, bacon, beans, sugar, and molasses.

As the town grew, the storekeeper sold more items. Sometimes, the storekeeper made items to sell in the store. One storekeeper built boats for his customers. Storekeepers got to know the people in the town so they knew what their customers wanted to buy.

LUNCH TIME

S torekeepers took a break for lunch when the store was quiet. The male and female storekeeper took turns eating lunch. This way, someone was always in the store to help customers.

After lunch, the storekeeper would deliver goods to people in town. The afternoon mail would then be picked up from the train station.

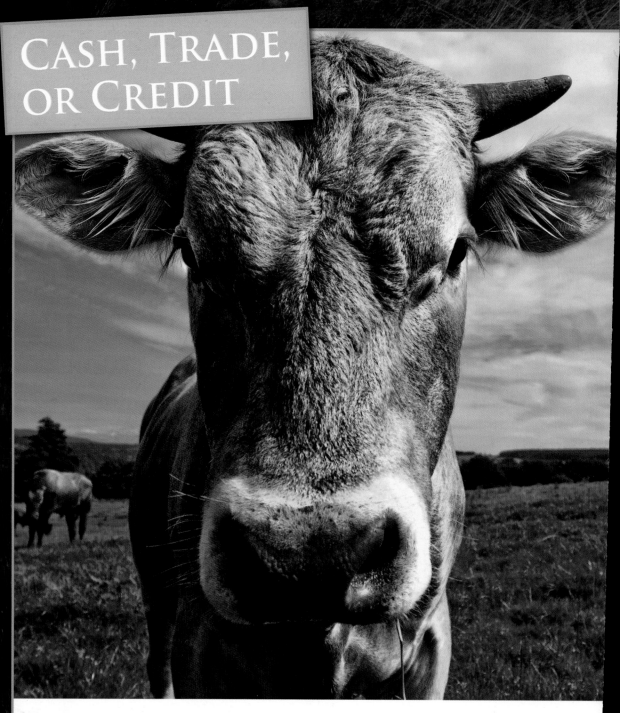

CASH, TRADE, OR CREDIT

Most storekeepers did not make much money. They ran their shops because they enjoyed working with the people in their community. Sometimes, settlers did not have money to pay for the items they needed. Instead, they might offer the storekeeper things such as butter, eggs, or even cows. This is called **bartering**.

S torekeepers gave some people store credit. They made a note in an account book and waited for the customer to pay when he or she could. Sometimes, storekeepers waited a year until a farmer harvested his crop. This store credit kept the settler's families from going hungry.

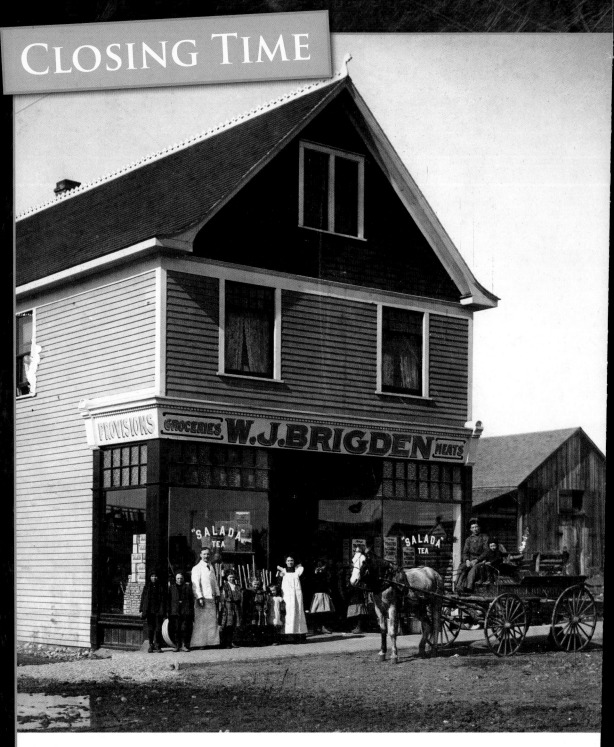

Often, a storekeeper's family helped in the store. A large family meant the storekeeper had many workers. At 4:00 pm, the storekeeper's children came home from school. The children dusted, swept the floors, and restocked the shelves.

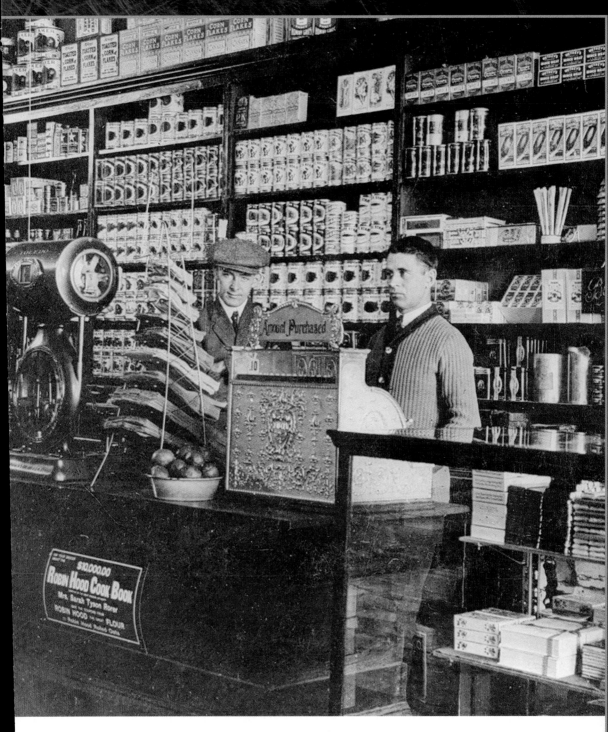

Customers might be in the shop at dinner time, so the family took turns eating their meal. The storekeeper would often keep the store open late to help customers.

CHRISTMAS

C hristmas was a busy time for storekeepers as people got ready for the holiday. They sold special items to give as gifts, such as dolls, story books, games, and candy. Settlers bought special items for baking, such as raisins or nuts. They also bought special foods for their holiday dinners.

The storekeeper decorated for Christmas and often had a Christmas tree in the store. The store window was a good place to show new toys and gifts. There was also more mail during the Christmas season. The extra letters and parcels kept the storekeeper busy.

STOREKEEPERS

Today, shop owners work very differently than in Canada's early days. Large department stores are common today. These stores are run by managers who do not own the store. The owners and managers hire many people to work in the store, not just family. Like the early storekeepers, these managers want to sell items that people need. Some of their tools are the same. Cash registers and scales are now electronic, like computers. Customers can still buy items on credit and pay for them later. Today, people use credit cards to do this.

Then and Now Diagram

DIAGRAM

Owning a shop in pioneer days was very different from modern times. The diagram on the right compares these differences and similarities. Copy the diagram in your notebook. Try to think of similarities and differences to add to your diagram.

THEN

- picked up and delivered mail
- traded goods for items such as eggs or butter
- lived in the back of the store
- relied on family to work in the store

- use cash registers
- let customers buy items using credit
- sell items customers need
- sell special items at Christmas

NOW

- rely on computers and scanners
- rarely know their customers
- hire many people to work in the store
- take only money, credit cards, or debit cards as payment

GLOSSARY

bartering: trading items for other items

bulk: items that must be weighed or measured, such as flour or nails

false front: the front of a building which is larger than the actual building

goods: items for sale

hub: central point of activity

inventory: a list of goods in the store

INDEX

account book 9, 17

community 6, 16

customer 9, 10, 11, 13, 14, 19,
       22, 23

goods 4, 5, 8, 9, 12, 15, 23

store 4, 5, 6, 7, 8, 9, 10, 11, 13,
       14, 17, 18, 19, 21, 22, 23